Cries of

Dr Paul Sheppy has written extensively in the areas of death and bereavement.

He is a local church minister and he lives in Reading.

Cries of the Heart

**A daily companion for your
journey through grief**

Paul Sheppy

CANTERBURY
PRESS
Norwich

© Paul Sheppy 2005

First published in 2005 by the
Canterbury Press Norwich
(a publishing imprint of Hymns Ancient &
Modern Limited, a registered charity)
9–17 St Albans Place, London N1 0NX

www.scm-canterburypress.co.uk

British Library Cataloguing in Publication data

A catalogue record for this book is available
from the British Library

ISBN 1-85311-669-6

Printed in Great Britain by
Bookmarque, Croydon, Surrey

Contents

Introduction

Neither death, nor life, nor angels, nor rulers, nor things present, nor things to come, nor powers, nor height, nor depth, nor anything else in all creation, will be able to separate us from the love of God in Christ Jesus our Lord.

Romans 8.38—39

This little book is intended to help those who are faced with the death of someone they love – whether that person has yet to die, has just died, or has died some time ago. At times like these there are no easy answers; but in the quiet of our own room, or with a few friends or family members, the memories linger – whether they are sweet or sharp. When tears come, it is good to be reminded that 'love needs watering', that our sense of loss is natural and that we need not be embarrassed.

Death comes in many ways. It may linger or be sudden; it may be violent or peaceful. It may be an unexpected or unimaginable shock; it may be the long-awaited end. However it comes, it always brings change; nothing will ever be quite the same, for someone who lived and moved and had their being among us is no longer here.

The prayers and readings in this book can be used whether you are alone or with friends. They are intended for private rather than public use, but you should use them in whatever way helps you most. Remember only this: that you do not talk to an empty room. The Christian story speaks of a parent (God) whose child (Jesus) dies in the most dreadful circumstances. If we remember that grief is an experience known by God, we will find ourselves talking to a sympathetic listener; and into the seeming silence we can pour our most secret thoughts – whether of anger and despair or of thankfulness and relief.

Nothing we can do or say will make God love us more; nothing we can do or say will make God love us less.

Do not let your hearts be troubled. Believe in God, believe also in me.

John 14.1

2

Framework

There are many ways of marking the process of bereavement. This book explores three different examples.

Part One, *The Forty Days*, is a sequence of forty days. The Italian word for 'forty' is *quarantina* (from which we get the word 'quarantine'). Each day has a scripture reading, a short thought and a prayer. The forty days cover three main areas of bereavement:

— taking leave;
— coping with uncertainty;
— starting afresh.

In this journey, we use scripture, quiet reflection and prayer to help us as we make our way. You may find it helpful to set aside a special time each day so that you can mark and trace the road.

Part Two, *Days of Remembrance*, contains prayers and meditations for various anniversaries and special occasions (birthdays, Christmas, New Year, and the like). Beyond the initial time of loss, there are special days that can easily bring it all back. Rather than allowing these times to plunge us into the depths, we can take the opportunity to take time with God to give thanks for the past and to set a course for the future.

Part Three, *Out of the Depths*, offers cries of the heart for varying circumstances of death and bereavement. You may find it helpful to use this section of the book as and when you feel the need to confront the special circumstances of the one whose death you are marking.

Do not let this book become a rigid set of exercises you must perform in a definite order. Use it like a road map to help you find your way with God through the time after the death of another.

Each day, each night, may God be your refuge and the close companion of your journey.

The Forty Days

The Forty Days: Introduction

Bereaved people are often told that it will take time to 'get back to normal'. Certainly, life after the death of someone we have loved can be hard to predict – we suddenly start to weep, or we find ourselves talking to the one we have lost. Yet it is not the same for everyone. Some people find it easier than others to deal with the initial period of loss.

It may be that the main feeling you have is that there is no feeling; you are numb and you simply cannot take it in. This does not mean that you are insensitive or unfeeling; numbness is a normal way of coping with shock. It may be taking time for things to sink in. If you don't seem to be feeling very much, don't reproach yourself; don't tell yourself that you couldn't really have cared. Your body is giving you time to come to terms with what has happened; use the space you are being granted to be quiet. The old advice to those living through dark days holds good: *Be still, and know that I am God.*

On the other hand, you may be feeling extremely raw. Death has come suddenly – perhaps too suddenly for proper goodbyes to have been said. Or you have been separated by distance and you could not get there in time. Maybe you are angry or bitter. Why has this happened to this person, and why now? You may even be looking for someone to blame: a driver in a road accident, or a doctor in the operating theatre, perhaps. Can you speak of these things to God, whose son, Jesus, was left alone to be butchered to death? At such times, the cry from the cross may speak for you: *My God, my God, why have you abandoned me?*

Yet again, you may be feeling relieved and thankful that one you have loved is no longer suffering. You do not wish them dead; but even more you did not wish them to go on enduring the life of their last days any longer. In your heart of hearts, you may even be glad that it is over. The burden of hospital visits or of daily care in the home has taken all your strength and sometimes may have left you feeling irritable with how things have turned out. You had planned to share retirement with your partner in better ways, and dementia or disease left them a shell of the person they were. Their decline drained you as well; and sometimes the thought climbed into your head that this was not fair, that you couldn't go on like this much longer yourself. Do not tell yourself that you are wicked, or that you are a failure. Sit quietly, and as you give thanks for better times and all that was good, hear the old words and find their comfort: *In returning and rest you shall be saved; in quietness and in trust shall be your strength.*

However, all this still begs the question: Can we get back to normal? At a deep level, the answer has to be 'No' – and for two reasons. First, the old 'normal' can never be repeated, for the one we love has gone. So, whatever we once counted as normality can never be the same again. Second, God calls us to a new way of life – the living and the dead. For them, life moves into a dimension where *we shall know as we are known*'; for us, the call is to live in the sure and certain hope of the resurrection. For us both, the past

8

becomes a gateway to a new awareness and experience of God's presence.

Through the forty days, we journey with God. Not every day's readings and prayer will perhaps capture your mood.

If you have been expecting this death for a long time, you may be feeling relief – both for the one who has died and for yourself. The mood of some readings may be too dark, too sombre.

If death has been sudden or untimely, some of the readings may feel too easy, too quick in offering hope.

Do not blame yourself for feeling as you do, but try gently to enter into the promises of God for you and for those we mourn. Do not allow your feelings to be the only measure of your living. By taking time to be with God, draw on resources that you never dreamed of knowing. Take your stand on the rock.

As you remember one who has died, this part of the book ends with the old prayer *In Paradisum* which asks that God's great welcome should be known by the one we remember.

Day 1

May those who sow in tears
reap with shouts of joy.

Psalm 16.5

A THOUGHT
Shall I weep till tears are no more
or wake from this heavy emptiness?
Shall I never hear that voice again?
Or shall I in this silence drown?

A PRAYER
O God,
joy is far away.
Joy is impossible.
In this solemn moment
give me the joy of your presence.

Day 2

Listen to me, O house of Jacob,
all the remnant of the house of Israel,
who have been borne by me from your birth,
carried from the womb;
even to your old age I am he,
even when you turn grey I will carry you.
I have made, and I will bear;
I will carry and will save.

Isaiah 46.3–4

A THOUGHT
Death comes for us whether we are old or young;
but in our death, God comes too. From what we
call our beginning to what we call our end, God is
not absent. In this moment, God will carry us –
the living and the dead – and in that carrying we
find our rescue.

A PRAYER
There are no words that we can say
that say enough;
there is no silence that we can keep
that is deep enough;
there is no gesture that we can make
that is enough.

So speak, O God,
say the word that is indeed enough.

Carry me, O God,
into the silence that stills anxiety,
forgives the past,
and calms my heart.

Day 3

Let your tears fall for the dead,
and as one in great pain begin the lament.
Lay out the body with due ceremony,
and do not neglect the burial.
Let your weeping be bitter
and your wailing fervent;
make your mourning worthy of the departed;
then be comforted for your grief.
When the dead is at rest,
let his remembrance rest too,
and be comforted for him
when his spirit has departed.

Ecclesiasticus 38.16–17, 23

A THOUGHT
The business of preparing the funeral can be
taxing on emotion. If you have friends who can
help you, do not be afraid to ask them. Planning to
say farewell properly and with dignity is an
important expression of love and respect. Do not
attempt too much.

What looks good in films and soaps has been
rehearsed by professional actors, using other
people's lines and in pretence. What you must do
is real and personal. Acknowledge and understand
the difference.

A PRAYER
O God,
there is so much to do;
grant me good friends and wise advice.
In all bustle and business,
give me a quiet mind and heart.
Through the tears and the smiles,
keep me sane, hold me safe.

Day 4

Jesus said:
'I am the resurrection and the life. Those who
believe in me, even though they die, will live, and
everyone who lives and believes in me will never
die. Do you believe this?' Mary said to him, 'Yes,
Lord, I believe that you are the Messiah, the Son
of God, the one coming into the world.'

John 11.25–27

A *THOUGHT*

These words were spoken on the fourth day of
the death of Mary's brother, Lazarus. Today is the
fourth day. Perhaps Mary's faith is greater than
ours. Even so, the words of Jesus do not change.
His promise remains.

A *PRAYER*

O God,
show me what life beyond death
can mean for me,
as I live my life
beyond the death of the one I remember now.

Day 5

Jesus said:
'Come to me, all you that are weary and are carrying heavy burdens, and I will give you rest. Take my yoke upon you, and learn from me; for I am gentle and humble in heart, and you will find rest for your souls. For my yoke is easy, and my burden is light.'

Matthew 11.28–30

A THOUGHT

When the burden seems heavy, when the
loneliness seems intense, when the loss seems too
much to bear – then hear the words of Jesus, who
offers to carry this burden with you, to enter into
the loneliness, to endure with you the loss.

Today is no longer impossible; others have walked
this way before you – and one, the Son of God,
comes to walk it with you.

A PRAYER

You have promised, O God,
you have promised.
Do not let me down;
give me strength enough for today.
Live with me, in me, through me.

Day 6

Out of the depths I cry to you, O LORD.
Lord, hear my voice!
Let your ears be attentive
to the voice of my supplications!
If you, O LORD, should mark iniquities,
Lord, who could stand?
But there is forgiveness with you,
so that you may be revered.
I wait for the LORD, my soul waits,
and in his word I hope;
my soul waits for the Lord
more than those who watch for the morning.

Psalm 130.1–6

A THOUGHT

Watching can be lonely and can feel empty. In the hours of quiet watching, fears and anxieties may come. We cannot stop their unbidden arrival, but we can face them with God. As with God we face what haunts or worries us, we find that however strong our feelings may be God is a match for them.

When we find ourselves struggling to cope, we turn to God who forgives and frees us and those we love from the past that tries to overwhelm us.

A PRAYER

Stay with me, O God,
when watching and remembering is a lonely task.
Fill me with courage
and speak to quieten my troubled heart.

Day 7

So we do not lose heart. Even though our outer nature is wasting away, our inner nature is being renewed day by day. For this slight momentary affliction is preparing us for an eternal weight of glory beyond all measure, because we look not at what can be seen but at what cannot be seen; for what can be seen is temporary, but what cannot be seen is eternal.

For we know that if the earthly tent we live in is destroyed, we have a building from God, a house not made with hands, eternal in the heavens.

2 Corinthians 4.16 – 5.1

A THOUGHT
Our carefully laid plans for the future lie
shattered; our dreams and hopes have come to
nothing. We have been knocked down, but not
knocked out. God is here in the loss with me.

A PRAYER
Dear God,
keep me still enough for you to find me.
Keep me quiet enough for me to hear you.
Keep me from despair, from bitterness.
Hide me in your secret place.

Day 8

The wilderness and the dry land shall be glad,
the desert shall rejoice and blossom;
like the crocus it shall blossom abundantly,
and rejoice with joy and singing.
Strengthen the weak hands,
and make firm the feeble knees.
Say to those who are of a fearful heart,
'Be strong, do not fear!'
Then the eyes of the blind shall be opened,
and the ears of the deaf unstopped.

Isaiah 35.1–2a, 3–4a, 5

A THOUGHT
A week has gone already. The onward movement
of days points to a greater day: a new day of
God's new making, when what is desert now will
become a garden.
As well as a future hope, there is strength for
today. When all seems shaken and shaky, God
holds us firm and firmly.

A PRAYER
O God,
when all is parched and dry,
bring me to an oasis.
When all is quicksand,
lead me to the rock.
When I tremble,
hold me close.

Day 9

The steadfast love of the LORD never ceases,
his mercies never come to an end;
they are new every morning;
great is your faithfulness.
'The LORD is my portion,' says my soul,
'therefore I will hope in him.'
The LORD is good to those who wait for him,
to the soul that seeks him.
It is good that one should wait quietly
for the salvation of the LORD.

Lamentations 3.22–26

A THOUGHT
Sometimes this silence feels good; sometimes it feels empty, alien, threatening. Yet God is here.

On the wall of a Cologne cellar where Jews hid from the Gestapo, someone wrote these words:

> *I believe in the sun though it is late in rising.*
> *I believe in love though it is absent.*
> *I believe in God though he is silent.*

A PRAYER
Fill this silence with your presence, O God.
Fill this room with your peace.
Fill my heart with your comfort.
Fill my mind with your hope.

Day 10

O LORD, God of my salvation,
when, at night, I cry out in your presence,
let my prayer come before you;
incline your ear to my cry.

Psalm 88.1–2

A THOUGHT
I sleep and then I wake. Or sleep comes when I
should be awake. Waking and sleeping, my
thoughts leap back and forth and rest seems fitful.

In all the confusion I am not alone. The cards and
letters from friends are bittersweet; but better
this pain than empty silence.

Memories come with solace as well as pain. Thank
God for those who care enough to sit with me
and remember with me and pray with me and for
me.

A PRAYER
Sometimes in the tears, O God,
there comes a calmer thought,
there comes the memory of joy and gladness,
there comes unbidden a smile.
For the small mercies,
make me thankful.
In the restless moments,
grant me peace.

Day 11

O LORD, you have searched me and known me.
You know when I sit down and when I rise up;
you discern my thoughts from far away.
You search out my path and my lying down,
and are acquainted with all my ways.
Even before a word is on my tongue,
O LORD, you know it completely.
If I say, 'Surely the darkness shall cover me,
and the light around me become night,'
even the darkness is not dark to you;
the night is as bright as the day,
for darkness is as light to you.

Psalm 139.1–4, 11–12

A THOUGHT
God knows and understands us. The desperation that drives us to run in the bad times and the frustration that hems us in so that we cannot escape – these times of darkness, when we cannot see the way ahead, do not blind God. God sees in and through the darkest night. The road we cannot find is known to the one who leads us from death to life, from despair to hope.

A PRAYER
O God,
when I cannot see the way forward,
teach me to trust you.
When I want to run,
be waiting to be my refuge.
When I am in the dark,
be my light.

Day 12

The LORD is my shepherd, I shall not want.
He makes me lie down in green pastures;
he leads me beside still waters;
he restores my soul.
He leads me in right paths for his name's sake.
Even though I walk through the darkest valley,
I fear no evil;
for you are with me
your rod and your staff –
they comfort me.
You prepare a table before me
in the presence of my enemies;
you anoint my head with oil;
my cup overflows.
Surely goodness and mercy shall follow
me all the days of my life,
and I shall dwell in the house of the LORD my
whole life long.

Psalm 23

A THOUGHT

This journey is a dark one, yet I do not travel alone. The same God who journeys with the one I love leads me. The same comfort strengthens us – the living and the dead.

There is food for the journey and no enemy (real or imagined) can steal what God is giving to sustain me.

A PRAYER

Give me strength enough for today, O God; give me food enough for the journey; and when my cup seems full of sorrow, drink it with me.

Day 13

Jesus said:
'I am the good shepherd. The good shepherd lays down his life for the sheep. The hired hand, who is not the shepherd and does not own the sheep, sees the wolf coming and leaves the sheep and runs away – and the wolf snatches them and scatters them. The hired hand runs away because a hired hand does not care for the sheep. I am the good shepherd. I know my own and my own know me.'

John 10.11–14

A THOUGHT
God does not run out on me or on the one I
mourn. We are each secure in God's faithful,
loving keeping.

When the wolf howls at the door of my heart,
when my mind is shaken by the night-time cry,
God stands between me and all that threatens my
peace.

I am safe.

A PRAYER
Time seems strange, O God.
Some days fly by;
others drag.
Some days, I almost feel nothing;
others, I ache through and through.
Keep me from the wolf that howls;
do not desert me,
but be my good shepherd.

Day 14

In returning and rest you shall be saved;
in quietness and in trust shall be your strength.
The LORD waits to be gracious to you;
he will rise up to show mercy to you.
For the LORD is a God of justice;
blessed are all those who wait for him.

Isaiah 30.15b, 18

A THOUGHT

Saying goodbye is like closing a chapter; it does not mean that we no longer remember, but that the present is different from the past. Conflicting emotions can become disturbing; what is needed is stability. However, we do not necessarily achieve that stability by using our will-power.

What we need is a place to which we can return and find peace. Various things may help us: photographs and videos; a quiet corner or place that holds good memories; or a time of day when we can be uninterrupted.

Such a place of recollection becomes healing when we allow God to dwell there with us. Then we can recall the past without being condemned to live in it. We will never want to forget; we will always need peace for today and tomorrow.

A PRAYER

O God,
meet me in the secret place
and give me the peace I long for.

Day 15

For old age is not honoured for length of time,
or measured by number of years;
but understanding is grey hair for anyone,
and a blameless life is ripe old age.
God's grace and mercy are with his elect,
and he watches over his holy ones.

Wisdom 4.8–10a, 15

A MEDITATION

When someone dies earlier than we expected, we sorrow the more. And, in one sense, we do so rightly.

Yet there is another perspective we may take without belittling our loss: God does not see time as we do. However old we are, there is more to do. However young we are, God waits to do new things with us. Death grieves us because we see it as the end. God opens a door, so that death and grief become paths to something new.

A PRAYER
O God,
death is mysterious
and beyond it we cannot see.
In the uncertainty of not knowing,
of not seeing,
bring us to the mystery
of your undying love and presence.

Day 16

Hear my cry, O God;
listen to my prayer.
From the end of the earth I call to you,
when my heart is faint.
Lead me to the rock that is higher than I;
for you are my refuge,
a strong tower against the enemy.

Psalm 61.1–3

A THOUGHT
The days pass and some things fade, while others remain sharp. The smallest thing may overturn a balance delicately achieved.

What is normal keeps changing and there is no going back, days run onward and each makes its claim. When the friends seem insensitive, or the world seems too distant or too close, find time to find the rock where you can stand firm.

A PRAYER
O God,
when I tremble,
be my refuge;
when I shake,
be my rock.

Day 17

Then I saw a new heaven and a new earth; for the
first heaven and the first earth had passed away,
and the sea was no more. And I heard a loud
voice from the throne saying,
> 'See, the home of God is among mortals.
> He will dwell with them as their God;
> they will be his peoples,
> and God himself will be with them;
> he will wipe every tear from their eyes.
> Death will be no more;
> mourning and crying and pain will be no more,
> for the first things have passed away.'

And the one who was seated on the throne said,
'See, I am making all things new.' Also he said,
'Write this, for these words are trustworthy and
true.'

Revelation 21.1, 3–5a

A THOUGHT
Why was there no more sea?

Because the sea is restless, uncontrollable, the mythic home of chaos. In God's making beyond death, the things that threaten to overwhelm us have no place.

For the one who journeys without us, there is a stability that provides a true homecoming. For us, who travel on without the one we now remember, the promise is the same: God is making a new world for us.

A PRAYER
O God,
do not let me sink in the sea of my sorrows;
set my feet on solid ground.
Do not let my tears overwhelm me;
take my hand and lead me on.

Day 18

All people are grass,
their constancy is like the flower of the field.
The grass withers, the flower fades;
but the word of our God will stand forever.
Have you not known? Have you not heard?
The LORD is the everlasting God,
the Creator of the ends of the earth.
He does not faint or grow weary;
his understanding is unsearchable.
He gives power to the faint,
and strengthens the powerless.
Even youths will faint and be weary,
and the young will fall exhausted;
but those who wait for the LORD
shall renew their strength,
they shall mount up with wings like eagles,
they shall run and not be weary,
they shall walk and not faint.

Isaiah 40.6–8, 28–31

A THOUGHT
Life seems so fragile when death appears; even memory seems unreliable and fading. In the face of death's finality, what had seemed permanent now is seen to be passing. Even the determination to keep going may falter.

When energy flags and determination is not enough, God comes to give us strength and to show us what truly endures.

A PRAYER
O God,
when I am weary, bring your strength;
when I feel lost, bring your direction;
when I am anxious, bring your wisdom.
Give me stamina,
give me courage,
give me rest.

Day 19

Jesus said:
I will not leave you orphaned; I am coming to you.
In a little while the world will no longer see me,
but you will see me; because I live, you also will
live.
Peace I leave with you; my peace I give to you. I
do not give to you as the world gives. Do not let
your hearts be troubled, and do not let them be
afraid.

John 14.18–19, 27

A *THOUGHT*
When the mind races or is shadowed by grief, it is hard to find peace. When a love has been lost, it is hard to find friendship.

Now is the time to turn to the source of all peace and the giver of a new intimacy, a deeper companionship.

A *PRAYER*
O God,
do not leave me alone with sorrow,
do not abandon me to empty thought.
Grant me
an awareness of your presence,
and the comfort of your love and peace.

Day 20

Now to him who is able to keep you from falling,
and to make you stand without blemish in the
presence of his glory with rejoicing, to the only
God our Saviour, through Jesus Christ our Lord,
be glory, majesty, power, and authority, before all
time and now and forever. Amen.

Jude 24–25

A THOUGHT

The days stumble past and we stumble through them. Questions keep asking themselves, and answers seem empty, pointless or absent. When all seems to be lost and stumbling becomes tumbling, there is one who holds us from the brink.

A PRAYER

O God,
keep me from falling,
keep me from empty regret,
keep me from demanding too much of myself.
Bring me to the place
where I am safe,
where I no longer stumble.

Day 21

Those of steadfast mind you keep in peace –
in peace because they trust in you.
Trust in the LORD forever,
for in the LORD GOD
you have an everlasting rock.

Isaiah 26.3–4

A THOUGHT
As the days pass, quietness of heart comes —
perhaps slowly, perhaps more quickly. The
sharpness of loss may be a little less intense.
There is no disloyalty in this; nor, when other
moments come, is there any failure.
The gift of God is to bring us to a new sense and
place of balance.

A PRAYER
For days when I cope,
O God,
I give my thanks.
For friends who call or write,
who visit or send their love —
for the standing firm,
O God,
I thank you.

51

Day 22

Now we see in a mirror, dimly, but then we will see face to face. Now I know only in part; then I will know fully, even as I have been fully known. And now faith, hope, and love abide, these three; and the greatest of these is love.

1 Corinthians 13.12–13

A THOUGHT
Days come when everything seems uncertain –
even faith. Days come when hope fades. Love
remains.

When everything else is puzzling, love remains.
And the love of God for us remains for ever.

A PRAYER
The love I have known,
O God,
holds me fast.
Root it deep in me,
let it grow in me,
let it fruit in me.
When all else is unclear,
let your gift of love shine within.

Day 23

The souls of the righteous are in the hand of God,
and no torment will ever touch them.
In the eyes of the foolish
their departure was thought to be a disaster,
and their going from us to be their destruction;
but they are at peace.
Those who trust in him will understand truth,
and the faithful will abide with him in love,
because grace and mercy are upon his holy ones,
and he watches over his elect.

Wisdom 3.1–3, 9

A THOUGHT
It is not for us to judge the lives of others – either
for good or for ill. The task for us is to remember
and to pray that as we in our turn come to death
we may have lived in justice and peace and love of
friend and stranger, making none our enemy. Here
is glory now and the best remembrance of those
who have died before us.

A PRAYER
O God,
give the peace you have promised
to the one I remember.
Give the peace you have promised
to me.
Teach me in small things to trust you,
so that in this great thing
I may hold firm.

Day 24

The LORD sets the prisoners free;
the LORD opens the eyes of the blind.
The LORD lifts up those who are bowed down;
the LORD loves the righteous.
The LORD watches over the strangers;
he upholds the orphan and the widow.

The LORD will reign forever,
your God, O Zion, for all generations.
Praise the LORD!

Psalm 146.6–9b, 10

A THOUGHT

If before we had always relied upon the one we now remember, it may feel as though we are defenceless. Bereavement really does leave us bereft in such circumstances.

Yet God is revealed to be the champion of those who have no one else to help them. Take the kindly words of friends as the gift of God and draw strength from an unlimited resource.

A PRAYER
O God,
fill this empty room,
fill this empty day,
fill my empty heart.

Open my eyes to your kindness,
open my mouth to your praise.

Day 25

O that my words were written down!
O that they were inscribed in a book!
O that with an iron pen and with lead
they were engraved on a rock forever!
For I know that my Redeemer lives.

Job 19.23–25a

A THOUGHT
Days come when everything seems to conspire against us, when even friends seem unfeeling. At such time we need someone who will stand with us through thick and thin – someone who will listen when others are unsympathetic or too busy.

Speak to God, who will not let your words disappear or your hurt go unnoticed.

When even that comfort seems absent, call on God to witness.

A PRAYER
Listen to me,
O God,
when will I find
what I look for?
Listen to me,
and answer my cry.

Day 26

Beloved, we are God's children now; what we will be has not yet been revealed. What we do know is this: when he is revealed, we will be like him, for we will see him as he is.

1 John 3.2

A THOUGHT
The death of another brings us face to face with our own future death. We ask ourselves the truly big questions – the questions to which we have no answer outside of God. Without God, there is no future. With God, the future is beyond our dreaming, our imagining.

We shall be as God is – that is the promise. Dare we trust?

A PRAYER
O God,
when my reason leads me to a blank wall;
lead me beyond reason.
When my certainty brings me to an abyss;
take me beyond certainty.
When my sense of who I am is changed;
transform me into the image of your Son.

Day 27

When I saw him, I fell at his feet as though dead.
He placed his right hand on me, saying, 'Do not be
afraid; I am the first and the last, and the living
one. I was dead, and see, I am alive forever and
ever; and I have the keys of Death and of Hades.'
Revelation 1.17–18

A THOUGHT

The experience of loss can suddenly assail us with extraordinary power. We feel overwhelmed by some small event or incident that we cannot predict or control. At such times, we feel as though we are about to fall through a crack in the earth.

In these moments, take time to recollect the power of God who touches us to still our fears and strengthen our hearts and minds.

A PRAYER

O God,
when my world starts to collapse,
when my life seems to be falling apart,
speak in the silence,
touch me in the eye of the storm,
and give me courage
to face such days, such times.

Day 28

I lift up my eyes to the hills –
from where will my help come?
My help comes from the LORD,
who made heaven and earth.
He will not let your foot be moved;
he who keeps you will not slumber.
He who keeps Israel
will neither slumber nor sleep.
The LORD is your keeper;
the LORD is your shade at your right hand.
The sun shall not strike you by day,
nor the moon by night.
The LORD will keep you from all evil;
he will keep your life.
The LORD will keep
your going out and your coming in
from this time on and forevermore.

Psalm 121

A *THOUGHT*
At times we do not know whether we are coming
or going; yet our coming and our going are kept
safe in God's hands. Sometimes the journey
appears unclear; yet our feet are kept from
slipping as God holds us – even in the most
difficult of circumstances.

A *PRAYER*
Hold on to me, O God,
when I fear that I may fall.
In the safety of your firm grip,
keep me looking upwards, onwards,
as I travel each day with you.

Day 29

Set your minds on things that are above, not on things that are on earth, for you have died, and your life is hidden with Christ in God. When Christ who is your life is revealed, then you also will be revealed with him in glory.

Colossians 3.2–4

A THOUGHT

As days slip past, it may be a little easier to 'let go and let God'. God's love and God's promise do not change when good days become dark. God my be trusted because when we stand in faith, we stand on the rock that is God – a solid ground beneath our feet.

There are no quick answers, but day by day we journey toward the life that is hidden in God.

A PRAYER
O God,
teach me how to let go
without forgetting.
Teach me how to live today
while being thankful for yesterday.
Teach me to walk into the future
with you.

Day 30

Jesus said:
'Very truly, I tell you, the hour is coming, and is
now here, when the dead will hear the voice of
the Son of God, and those who hear will live.'

John 5.25

A THOUGHT
Death seems to end in silence, but a new hearing
becomes possible. As the insistent noise of our
world fades, the voice of the Son of God makes
itself heard. What we so often fail to hear now
becomes startlingly clear.

For me, the many voices compete for my
attention. For the one I remember, one voice
alone is heard; and that voice calls all who hear to
life.

A PRAYER
As I let go, O God,
hold fast to the one I love
and hold me fast in your love.
Speak your word of life
and help me to hear it
in the duties and tasks of today.
When I hear,
make me trustful.

Day 31

The righteous live forever,
and their reward is with the Lord;
the Most High takes care of them.
Therefore they will receive a glorious crown
and a beautiful diadem from the hand of the Lord,
because with his right hand he will cover them,
and with his arm he will shield them.

Wisdom 5.15–16

A Thought

The righteous one, above all others, is Jesus. His death is for us and his resurrection is for us. None of us is perfect. We find our hope and opportunity of being made perfect in what Jesus has done.

If we can entrust ourselves to that, then as God looks at us it is through the lens of Jesus. The crown that is his becomes ours also. God becomes a shield to us rather than a threat. The love we see in God puts our fears to flight.

A Prayer
O God,
when I am fearful –
for myself,
for those I love,
for the one I remember –
be my shield
and crown me with your love.

Day 32

They will hunger no more, and thirst no more;
the sun will not strike them,
nor any scorching heat;
for the Lamb at the centre of the throne
will be their shepherd,
and he will guide them
to springs of the water of life,
and God will wipe away
every tear from their eyes.

Revelation 7.16–17

A THOUGHT

That their suffering is at an end, that the one we remember is at peace – this can be the doorway to our own quietening. As we come to terms with what has happened, we begin to move forward with purpose and, yes, even with hope.

A PRAYER

O God,
when I weep only for myself,
wipe the tears from my eyes.
When I think only of the thirst that I endure,
lead me to the fountain of others' tears.
Wash me there with a sympathy
that strengthens them
for today
and tomorrow.

Day 33

How long, O LORD?
Will you forget me forever?
How long will you hide your face from me?
How long must I bear pain in my soul,
and have sorrow in my heart all day long?
How long shall my enemy be exalted over me?

Psalm 13.1–2

A *THOUGHT*
Every time I think that I may be recovering a little,
something comes to remind me.

I see someone walking in the street; I hear a
familiar laugh. Suddenly, everything comes to a
stop.

At times, the pain seems unbearable; I do not
know how I will cope. At other times, everything
seems so normal; I wonder if I have imagined it.

In all times, God comes close enough to hear me,
to carry me, to hold me – if only I am willing.

A *PRAYER*
How long does this go on, O God?
Shall I ever be the same?
Or are you calling me to be made new?
Make me willing!

Day 34

Look, I have set before you an open door, which no one is able to shut. I know that you have but little power.

Revelation 3.8

A *THOUGHT*

When we feel weak or unable to keep going, this word comes. God knows and understands, and opens the door, wedging it in position. No one can shift it or close it.

You do not have to push. Just walk through. The future is lit by the love of God who wipes away our tears.

A *PRAYER*

This door, O God?
Through this door?
How shall I know where it goes?
Lead me through it
and conquer my fears.
Give me today
the courage to make the step
and the calm that comes
in following you.

Day 35

Now may the God of peace, who brought back
from the dead our Lord Jesus, the great shepherd
of the sheep, by the blood of the eternal covenant,
make you complete in everything good so that
you may do his will, working among us that which
is pleasing in his sight, through Jesus Christ, to
whom be the glory forever and ever. Amen.

Hebrews 13.20–21

A THOUGHT

When thoughts wander and attention strays, we need a good and gentle shepherd to lead us back to careful remembrance and better living.

A PRAYER

O God,
I lose track of what I am doing,
of where I am.
Good intentions
are so soon forgotten,
and gentleness can so easily be lost
in irritation or self-pity.
Lead me back to better ways,
guide me to loving paths.

Day 36

'Where, O death, is your victory?
Where, O death, is your sting?'

The sting of death is sin, and the power of sin is
the law. But thanks be to God, who gives us the
victory through our Lord Jesus Christ.

1 Corinthians 15.55–57

A *THOUGHT*
It still sometimes feels as though death has won.
The physical absence of one we love is so real.
The old trick of a smile or a simple gesture has
gone. The crack of laughter, the outburst of
frustration or anger, the flash of humour – all are
no longer anything other than remembered. It still
sometimes feels as though death has won.
The resurrection of Jesus teaches us that death
does not win. Life and love are not so easily
conquered, for they are the free and absolute gift
of God.

A *PRAYER*
O God,
when death seems to have won
because it is so final,
show me the greatness of love
that suffers to bring forth life
that no grave, no stone can hold.

Day 37

On this mountain
the LORD of hosts will make for all peoples
a feast of rich food,
a feast of well-aged wines,
of rich food filled with marrow,
of well-aged wines strained clear.
And he will destroy on this mountain
the shroud that is cast over all peoples,
the sheet that is spread over all nations;
he will swallow up death forever.
Then the Lord GOD will wipe away
the tears from all faces,
and the disgrace of his people
he will take away from all the earth,
for the LORD has spoken.
This is the LORD for whom we have waited;
let us be glad and rejoice in his salvation.

Isaiah 25.6–8, 9b

A THOUGHT

Feasting can seem so far away – it almost seems indecent to think about enjoying the richness and variety of life. Or it may seem impossible without the one whose memory you keep.

To our table God comes. At our table Christ breaks bread. Over our table the Spirit pours healing. The feast is not spread on a table of forgetfulness but of loving-kindness.

A PRAYER
O God,
when the past seeks to overwhelm me
with loss and sorrow,
grant me the future
you have promised.

Day 38

What no eye has seen, nor ear heard, nor the human heart conceived, what God has prepared for those who love him – these things God has revealed to us through the Spirit; for the Spirit searches everything, even the depths of God.

1 Corinthians 2.9

A T*HOUGHT*
Beyond human fears and imagining, beyond human
hopes and dreaming, lies the glory which God has
prepared. The resurrection of Jesus is not an old
fairy tale or an obscure piece of history. It is the
promise that God holds for all creation. Nothing
is lost; all will be transformed.

This includes those we have loved – and us, too.

A P*RAYER*
O God,
is such a future possible?
For *N*?
For me?
Teach me to live today
the new life you are shaping for all creation.

Day 39

Jesus said:
'I am the light of the world. Whoever follows me will never walk in darkness but will have the light of life.'

John 8.12

A THOUGHT

The journey is always from darkness to light. Even when the darkness deepens or seems total, God's answer is light.

Sometimes, it is simply light enough for the next step; and, as we take that step, the light moves on. Sometimes, the light reveals more.

Finally, the light is life – the transfigured life of those who walk by the light of God revealed in Jesus and shining within us by the Spirit. That light is promised to you. Take it and walk by it into the future that awaits and that God is making new.

A PRAYER

O God,
be for me light and hope and life itself.
Be for *N* resurrection light and life.
Be all in all for us all.

Day 40

Now, Lord, you let your servant go in peace:
your word has been fulfilled.
My own eyes have seen the salvation
which you have prepared
    in the sight of every people
a light to reveal you to the nations
and the glory of your people Israel.

The Song of Simeon, adapted from Luke 2.29–32

A THOUGHT
The journey is not over, but it is begun. Even
when I have been on my own, God has not left
me. There have been quiet words and memories,
the kindness of friends and neighbours – even
when the world has been a rush, a noise.

The blade of grass that pushes through the
concrete and the sun that slowly melts the ice
have been signs of hope and of new beginnings.

God's last word is not 'death', but 'life'.

A PRAYER
God of my journey,
travel with me into the days ahead.
Give me courage of heart,
peace of mind and quiet trust.
Bring light out of darkness,
hope out of despair, and life out of death.
For these days to grieve I thank you.
For the days to mend I praise you.
For what is to be I trust you.

In Paradisum

An ancient prayer from the Catholic tradition

May the angels lead you into paradise;
at your approach may the martyrs welcome you
and bring you to the holy city Jerusalem.
May the angel choir come to greet you,
and with Lazarus, who once was poor,
may you find eternal rest.

Days of Remembrance

Days of Remembrance: Introduction

Beyond the early days of bereavement lie the days that are special because they mark milestones in our continuing life. Among these are anniversaries and birthdays, and days that hold other particular memories.

In this section of the book there are readings and prayers to accompany these additional days of remembrance. Not all of these may be relevant to you. Or you may feel as though their initial turmoil is about to destroy the acceptance you have so painfully achieved. Use what feels helpful and look for pointers from the past that show you the way to God's good future.

Listen to some music that you shared, or look (if you can) at old photographs, or walk where once you walked together. Do not live in the past, but do not dishonour it by forgetting it. As memories flood back, give thanks to God for what was good and seek healing for anything that remains painful.

Of course, it may well be that there are times and days that you want to remember that are not covered here. For this reason, you will find the old Jewish prayer called *Kaddish*. It is a prayer praising God for the past and blessing God who is God alone to be praised and blessed. You may find it helpful to say this prayer from time to time as you establish new rhythms and patterns in your living.

It is good, when the early days have passed, to continue in the way that God grants to all who mourn: *Blessed are those who mourn, for they will be comforted* (Matthew 5.4).

The Day of the Funeral

Jesus said:
'Do not let your hearts be troubled. Believe in
God, believe also in me. In my Father's house
there are many dwelling places. If it were not so,
would I have told you that I go to prepare a place
for you? And if I go and prepare a place for you, I
will come again and will take you to myself, so that
where I am, there you may be also.'

John 14.1–3

TWO PRAYERS
The hour has come and now is,
when I must go where I would rather not.
Go before me, go beside me,
go behind me, go within me,
lead me to your eternal house
and make your dwelling with me.

> *adapted from* In Sure and Certain Hope

Thank you, O God,
for your presence today
in the words that spoke to my heart,
in the friends who held me tight,
in the silence of sympathy,
in the quietness of farewell spoken.

Birthday

And now bless the God of all,
who everywhere works great wonders,
who fosters our growth from birth,
and deals with us according to his mercy.
May he give us gladness of heart,
and may there be peace in our days
in Israel, as in the days of old.

Ecclesiasticus 50.22–23

A THOUGHT
Whether your own birthday or the birthday of
the one you remember, these days can be
bittersweet. Where possible, share some time
with a sympathetic friend who as well as listening
will help you to find ways forward as anniversaries
come and go.

Above all, find some time to be still enough to let
remembrance be brought into the presence of
God. Time passes, memories change and even
become hard to sustain; God stays with you in and
through it all.

A PRAYER
O God,
old memories are sweet;
do not let them choke me,
like a creeper round a tree.
Old memories are sweet,
do not let them become fruitless,
making me barren and bitter.
Stand beside me
and fill memory with your presence.
Dwell in me and root me in you.

Wedding Anniversary

Look, O daughters of Zion, at King Solomon,
at the crown with which his mother crowned him
on the day of his wedding,
on the day of the gladness of his heart.

Song of Songs 3.11

A Thought

Anniversaries of marriage or other significant days when love is remembered can be hard to approach. It is not always good to be alone at such times; a phone conversation or the visit of a friend may help. Sorrow shared may become sorrow more easily endured.

More importantly, do not hide from the presence of God. The one who is love and the giver of love knows the pain and cost of love. We are not alone.

A Prayer
O God,
this used to be a day of celebration,
let it still be a day of thankfulness.

Christmas

Joy and gladness are taken away
from the fruitful field;
and in the vineyards no songs are sung,
no shouts are raised;
no treader treads out wine in the presses;
the vintage-shout is hushed.
Therefore my heart throbs like a harp.

Isaiah 16.10–11a

A THOUGHT
There is a balance to be kept here. Christmas
without the one we remember can seem hard to
celebrate and we may feel a natural sadness while
others seem so loudly cheerful.

We need to remember that the Christmas story
remains the same. Beyond the tinsel and the
glitter and the feasting is the baby; and in the new
life, which itself will come to brutal death, there is
the seed of something exceeding all our hopes and
dreams.

Remember the one you mourn; remember, too,
the Christ-child.

A PRAYER
On this day,
O God,
all that you are
is found in the fragile life of a baby.
Let that life fill mine
and be the hope of all we remember at this time.

New Year's Day

As for mortals, their days are like grass;
they flourish like a flower of the field;
for the wind passes over it, and it is gone,
and its place knows it no more.
But the steadfast love of the LORD
is from everlasting to everlasting
on those who fear him,
and his righteousness to children's children.

Psalm 103.15–17

A THOUGHT
The start of a new year can be a difficult time. So
many people are celebrating in groups; and if the
remembered one was part of those celebrations,
there may be an emptiness which is felt in
heartache. Louise Haskins' words may come as a
source of quiet reassurance:

*I said to the man who stood at the gate of the year:
'Give me a light that I may tread safely into the
unknown.' And he replied: 'Go out into the darkness
and put your hand into the hand of God. That shall be
to you better than light and safer than a known way.'*

A PRAYER
O God,
when the future seems overshadowed by the past,
shine your light into my fearful heart
and let me know
that you are near.

Year's End or First Anniversary

Jesus said:
'This is the will of him who sent me, that I should lose nothing of all that he has given me, but raise it up on the last day. This is indeed the will of my Father, that all who see the Son and believe in him may have eternal life; and I will raise them up on the last day.'

John 6.39–40

A THOUGHT
A year has passed – perhaps swiftly, perhaps
slowly – and the markers along the way have been
placed and passed. They mark the future journey.
As I look back, I also look forward.

The God of my past is the God who leads me into
a future guaranteed by the resurrection of Jesus in
whose life my own is hidden.

A PRAYER
O God,
when memory is sad,
hold me gently in your hand.

When memory is sweet,
give me grace to thank you.

Watch always over *N*,
and at the last may I with *her*
understand and know your love.

adapted from In Sure and Certain Hope

All Souls' Day: 2 November

Let the same mind be in you that was in Christ
Jesus,
    who, though he was in the form of God,
    did not regard equality with God
    as something to be exploited,
    but emptied himself,
    taking the form of a slave,
    being born in human likeness.
    And being found in human form,
    he humbled himself
    and became obedient to the point of death –
    even death on a cross.
    Therefore God also highly exalted him
    and gave him the name
    that is above every name,
    so that at the name of Jesus
    every knee should bend,
    in heaven and on earth and under the earth,
    and every tongue should confess

that Jesus Christ is Lord,
to the glory of God the Father.

Philippians 2.5–11

A PRAYER
Eternal God,
you hold the keys of life and death,
and through the death of Jesus Christ,
you have opened the gates of glory.

Keep those we have remembered
in your eternal care,
and bring them to the feast of your new creation.

Deliver us from fear and doubt
and strengthen in us
the faith that brings us to your eternal presence.

Hear us for the sake of your Son, Jesus Christ,
who died and rose for all,
and who lives now, our great high priest.
To him and to you with the Holy Spirit
be glory and praise for ever.
Amen.

adapted from In Sure and Certain Hope

Kaddish

An ancient prayer from the Jewish tradition

Magnified and sanctified
may His great Name be
in the world that He created,
as He wills.
May His kingdom come
in your lives and in your days
and in the lives of all the house of Israel,
swiftly and soon;
and say all, Amen!

Amen!
May His great Name be blessed
always and forever!

Blessed
and praised
and glorified
and raised
and exalted

and honoured
and uplifted
and lauded
be the Name of the Holy One
(He is blessed!)
above all blessings
and hymns and praises and consolations
that are uttered in this world;
and say all, Amen!

May a great peace from heaven –
and life! –
be upon us and upon all Israel;
and say all, Amen!

May He who makes peace in His high places
make peace upon us and upon all Israel;
and say all, Amen!

Out of the Depths

Out of the Depths: Introduction

In this final part of the book, we acknowledge those circumstances of death that call from us particular depths of sorrow, which may be expressed in unutterable silence, inarticulate despair, or wildest grief.

The format changes here. There are not always scripture readings – for example, one reading from Jeremiah about Rachel weeping for her children precedes a group of four circumstances of death: stillbirth, perinatal death, the death of a child and the death of a young person. For other circumstances, there is simply a call upon God.

These cries from the depths are raw and unpolished. There is no polite way of saying that we hurt to the point of anger, frustration, despair or plain unbelief.

When this is how we feel, calm assurance means nothing. What we need is a companion with whom we can shout, a hate-figure at whom we can yell.

Take God as the one you trust; take God as the one you hate. But do not leave God out of the reckoning. Shout your anger; whisper your fear. But do not cease talking to God.

When the world is unending night and the heavens are unyielding bronze, try to hold to these words found on the wall of a cellar in Cologne where Jews had been hiding from the Gestapo:

> *I believe in the sun though it is late in rising.*
> *I believe in love though it is absent.*
> *I believe in God though he is silent.*

Rachel is Weeping

A voice is heard in Ramah,
lamentation and bitter weeping.
Rachel is weeping for her children;
she refuses to be comforted for her children,
because they are no more.

Jeremiah 31.15

Stillbirth

O God,
we longed for the life of a child,
and now our hopes are taken from us.
The emptiness is all we feel now;
the silence is all we hear.
Give us time, O God,
give us space,
give us yourself.

An Infant

We knew life was fragile.
We knew life was precious.

O God!
So fragile!
So precious!

No answer calls back life,
no explanation renews hope.

Say something
that tells us you are near,
you are here,
you are with us.

A Child

So many hopes, so many fears,
so much joy, so much sorrow;
and now all words seem empty.

What we want we cannot have;
and what we thought was promised
has been taken from us.

adapted from In Sure and Certain Hope

A Young Person

Father God,
who watched your own Son die,
our hearts ache beyond our describing –
they break and we feel beyond all comfort.
The heavens seem shut,
and the earth is a wilderness of sorrow and grief.
With your Son on his cross we cry,
My God, my God, why have you abandoned me?

taken from In Sure and Certain Hope

O God,
do not let pain turn to the bitterness
that devours us and kills us.
We thank you for all that was good.
Help us to find peace in troubled times,
and light in our darkness.

adapted from In Sure and Certain Hope

A Parent

Loving God,
be a *father/mother* to me,
as I remember one who loved and nurtured me.

Be for me
a place of refuge,
a rock in the storm,
a light in the darkness.

adapted from In Sure and Certain Hope

A Partner

Thank you that so much of life has been shared.

For all that was good
and fun and glad –
I give my thanks.

From what was hard
or difficult or sad –
give me grace to learn.

In laughter and tears,
In dreams realised,
in obstacles overcome,
in all that was done together –
gladness mingles with the sorrow.

Keep me true, O God,
to what was best in us
and to the gift of love we knew
and that death cannot sever.

For Everything there is a Season

For everything there is a season,
and a time for every matter under heaven:
a time to be born, and a time to die;
a time to plant,
and a time to pluck up what is planted – . . .
a time to break down, and a time to build up;
a time to weep, and a time to laugh;
a time to mourn, and a time to dance;
a time to throw away stones,
and a time to gather stones together;
a time to embrace,
and a time to refrain from embracing;
a time to seek, and a time to lose;
a time to keep,
and a time to throw away;
a time to tear, and a time to sew;
a time to keep silence, and a time to speak;
a time to love, and a time to hate;
a time for war, and a time for peace.

Ecclesiastes 3.1–8

Violent Death

Not this way,
O God, not this way.

Yet N is snatched away
and we are left with emptiness and anger,
with lostness and pain.

Speak to us in the resounding silence
and give us courage to face what remains.

Silence

Be to us a tower and shield;
grant to N welcome and peace.

Hear us, O God,
for your Son, too,
was a victim of violence.

adapted from In Sure and Certain Hope

Suicide

It is too hard to bear,
N's pain was more than *she* could stand;
and now we suffer pain – not *hers* but ours.

O God, *N* saw no other way out,
lead *her* now to the one
who bore his pain to death,
and grant *her* peace.

   adapted from In Sure and Certain Hope

Sudden Death

God of all time,
this time seems wrong, too soon.
Help me to believe
that this time
and all times
are your time.
On this day of grief
bear with us the pain of what has happened;
and give us the healing
of wounds that now run deep.

adapted from In Sure and Certain Hope

Dementia

O God,
we have seen this coming from afar.
For so many days *N* seemed remote,
and we lost *her* as *she* lost us.
Yet you have known us all,
and you have kept us all in your eternal love.
Welcome home the one we mourn,
the friend who became a stranger.
Grant to *her* the recognition of your face
and that life which never fades.

adapted from In Sure and Certain Hope

After Long Illness

God of all the years,
you hold the keys of life and death.
For *N* the journey was slow and hard,
the days of illness long and wearisome.
Lead *her* home now to you,
that *she* may rest
where pain and agony are no more
and where you wipe away all tears.
Be *her* eternal light,
and grant *her* to eat from the tree of life.

Thank you, O God,
for those who have cared for *N*
in these last days [over many days];
for their skill and their kindness,
for their watchful eye, their soothing hand.
Thank you for those
who brought relief from pain,
and shared our burden with us.

adapted from In Sure and Certain Hope

Natural Disaster

Where, O God, were you?
Did you not care?
Have you hidden from us all hope and believing?

Our hearts and minds reel,
our thoughts and speech outrun reason
and we cry out in pain.

O God, where are you?
Do not hide your face from us.
Do not leave us without comfort or solace.

When we run to the ends of the earth,
when we rage in the dark of the night,
meet us there,
and grant us peace and hope enough
to entrust *N* to you.
With all who suffer at this time we cry to you.

taken from In Sure and Certain Hope

Where there is no Body

O God,
saying goodbye is so hard.

Where is the one I remember?
Why could I not stand
where *she* lies?
How I long for some remembrance!

In the emptiness
of these days,
heal my aching heart.

My tears wash *her*;
wash me.

My arms long to touch *her* one last time;
hold us in your arms.

Index of Scriptures

Index of Scriptures

Quotations are from the
New Revised Standard Version.

Sources and
Acknowledgements

Sources and Acknowledgements

Several prayers have been taken and adapted from the author's previous publication *In Sure and Certain Hope* (SCM-Canterbury Press, 2003).

The ancient prayers, *In Paradisum* and *Kaddish*, are found in many translations.

Scripture quotations are from the New Revised Standard Version of the Bible, copyright 1989 by the Division of Christian Education of the National Council of the Churches of Christ in the USA. Used by permission. All rights reserved.

Thanks are due to Betty Brown for reading the typescript before it was sent to The Canterbury Press. She is thoroughness and cheerfulness combined – a wonderful blend.

To the staff at the Press my thanks are due for efficiency and care. To Christine Smith go my special thanks for her initial commission and her continuing encouragement.

I cannot end without recording my wife's calm acceptance of the way I write. Once more, Sue has endured interrupted nights and snatched suppers as I have pursued my apparently endless preoccupation with death and funerals.

I fear I shall never finish with death until death finishes with me.